Rainy
Day
Edinburgh

A Practical Guide:

100 Places to Keep Dry

Mike MacEacheran

Photography by
Alexander Baxter

Hardie Grant

QUADRILLE

North 33

Central 11

Introduction

Densely packed with galleries, museums and world-class institutions, but also crowned by a skyline dominated by steampunk spires, steeples and the crags of a 340-million-year-old volcanic plug, Edinburgh is extraordinary whether you're a first-timer or back for an extra helping. The setting itself is riddle-like, with a subterranean underbelly of webbed alleys and cobblestoned closes that zigzag through the Old Town like a giant game of snakes and ladders. Explore the wider cityscape from the New Town to Morningside to Portobello and beyond and you'll also find a city of superlative castles (few know Edinburgh actually has three...) and scores of destinations where you can lose yourself amid the rich traditions and stories of a city that has had a disproportionate influence on the worlds of art, architecture, literature, music and more. If anything, this is a city that encourages notions of the fantastic.

All of this comes with a caveat, of course. Edinburgh has many nicknames – Auld Reekie (Scots for Old Smoky) and Athens of the North are two popular ones, for instance – but, perhaps, the most fitting is the Windy City.

The capital is positioned between the North Sea coast and Pentland Hills, with the prevailing wind direction coming from the southwest and it brings with it unpredictable rain showers and glowering storm clouds. Which is to say hiding out in museums and art galleries on a rainy day is an art form here.

For food and dining out – the purest expression of any city – avoid the menus of haggis and out-of-the-freezer fish and chips on the Royal Mile and around the Grassmarket in the Old Town, and dig deeper into city life by heading northwest to Stockbridge or northeast to trend-setting Leith, which has both Edinburgh's most vibrant grassroots scene and more game-changing haute cuisine than anywhere else in Scotland. And the perfect partner to all that? Drink, of course. This is the home of single malt whisky after all – and Scots are equally proud of their hospitality and gin- and beer-making heritage – and nowhere in the country has as many buzzy cocktail bars and lavishly-appointed pubs as Edinburgh. You might go from a Victorian-era backstreet boozer in the Old Town to the slightly-macabre subterranean streets of the

Cowgate for a night of cocktails and decadence. Equally satisfying is a tour of the city's fledgling indie craft brewers.

Whether you've spotted this book while sheltering from a rain storm (all too common on the Scottish east coast, if truth be told), or are keen to get ahead with booking must-visit restaurants and museum exhibitions before an upcoming trip, consider this guide an introduction to a capital city that, though compact and easy to navigate, never stops to catch its breath. Either way, I hope these recommendations will reassure you that the Scottish capital is as brilliant a place to be on a rainy day as it is when that giant orange-yellow orb in the sky appears.

When to travel

Scotland is notorious for its inclement weather and there are dozens of words to describe the weather on overcast days. From 'dreich' (meaning dreary and bleak), to 'smirr' (fine drizzle) to 'bucketin'' (a downpour) to 'pure Baltic' (absolutely freezing), there's an urban myth that this is a country of 100 words for rain and bad weather.

And even though Edinburgh is on the drier, warmer east coast, it still gets its fair share of sullen skies, dramatic downpours and 'haars' (veiled sea mists rolling in from the east). Climate change also means it's harder to gauge monthly rainfall patterns, but if you're planning a trip, it can be helpful to have a rough idea of what might be in store depending on the time of year you're visiting.

The city has a temperate oceanic climate and on average the coldest months are January, February and December (highs of 6°C/42.8°F; lows of 1°C/33.8°F), while the warmest months are June, July and August (highs of 19°C/66.2°F; lows of 11°C/51.8°F). The city is also at its wettest in October (average monthly rainfall is 75mm/3 inches), July (70mm/2.8 inches) and August (70mm/2.8 inches). If you're hoping to swerve the storm clouds, the months with the lowest average rainfall are April and May, when there is as little as 40mm/1.6 inches of rain.

Considering Edinburgh is at 55°N, almost the same latitude as Moscow, it's hardly surprising it harbours cold, humid winters and mild summers.

About this book

While the 100 entries in this book offer a wonderful introduction to Scotland's capital city, the list is by no means exhaustive. Instead, this is a collection of rain-friendly in-the-know recommendations – the sorts of places I would recommend to friends. In these pages, you'll find a mix of heavyweights, like museums and cultural institutions, harder-to-find independent businesses and unmissable places that just can't be missed (no matter how obvious they might seem).

The chapters are divided roughly by geographical area – central, north, west, south, east. I've put Edinburgh Castle as the focal point of the Central chapter and worked outwards from there – in reality Leith is more to the north of the city, but it sits well with Portobello in the East chapter as an extension to the usual Edinburgh sights. A compact city – more so than many other powerhouse capitals – Edinburgh's hills make it harder to get around than you may at first think. Many places within the same chapter can be reached on foot, while others will be easier to get between by bus, tram or taxi.

Within each section, there are four categories: Cafés & Restaurants, Pubs & Bars, Art & Culture and Shops. These have been hand-picked with wet days in mind, which means they are all, of course, safe from the elements and indoors. And as rain showers turn up unexpectedly, the book does not include any activities that would require much forward planning.

To make things as simple as possible when flicking through these pages, particularly if you are on the go, there is also a key, which includes the following categories:

☺ **Family-friendly** This is a city almost masterplanned from the very beginning with children in mind. A fairy-tale castle? A volcano? A labyrinth of half-hidden streets? More parks and green spaces than any other city in the UK? There's all that and more, plus Edinburgh is home to numerous kid-friendly festivals and even provided the inspiration for Harry Potter – author J.K. Rowling lives in Cramond and wrote the wizarding saga in many of its cafés. As much as anything then, Edinburgh has dozens of terrific things to do with children, and you'll find some of the most intriguing within this book. If this symbol is included, it means there's something extra special for little ones or teens – it might be a restaurant that rolls out the red carpet for fussy eaters, or a museum or gallery with hands-on activities galore.

⊛ **Free** The lion's share of cultural institutions, museums and galleries in the city are gloriously free to visit – the downside, however, is many can pack out on wet days. The best museums and galleries frequently host special ticketed events and touring exhibitions that might include a separate entry fee. Check online before you visit.

🏠 **Booking ahead recommended** Most of the venues in this book accept reservations – hyped restaurants that demand patrons queue outside (often in the rain) are few and far between in Edinburgh. Most venues don't require a large amount of forward-planning to visit – the ones that do tend to be the city's most in-demand Michelin-star restaurants or late-night cocktail bars. Most places have online reservation systems, but if no availability is showing on a website, try calling up to have your name added to the waiting list – last-minute cancellations are far more common than restaurateurs would like. Otherwise, the only other times in Edinburgh you might want to book ahead are for special exhibitions at one of its world-beating museums or cultural institutions, or for the cinema.

Getting around

Public transport

Bus

If any capital city was created to be discovered in a comfy pair of waterproof shoes, it is Edinburgh. The Old and New Towns reveal their secrets best at street level and with your senses exposed to all the elements, but when it rains there's a high chance you'd want to get around without getting soaked. With that in mind, the best way to explore the four corners of the capital is by bus. The main operator you'd want to consider is Lothian Buses, which offers reliable and regular 24-hour bus services to all areas covered in this book.

A Lothian Buses Day Ticket (£4.50 at the time of writing) allows unlimited journeys on day services in the city centre. For detailed maps and bus schedules, visit lothianbuses.com. A useful app to have on your device is the Lothian Buses app, which shares live schedules, service alerts and tracks bus departures from every stop in the city – the system is designed to help you plot your journey across the city with minimal fuss. If you prefer to hold an actual map in your hands, there is a great selection of Edinburgh maps for sale at the bookshops listed in this guide.

Trams

While there is only one tram line in Edinburgh, it's a scenic and satisfying way to explore large parts of the city from west to east – namely Haymarket, the West End, Princes Street and the foot of Calton Hill at the east end of the city centre. Trams depart at least every 15 minutes from around 6am to 11pm, taking around half an hour. At the time of writing, tickets cost £6.50 from the airport and can be purchased from the machines or on board. Currently, the tram terminates in the east near the top of Leith Walk, but an extension to Ocean Terminal and The Shore in Leith is set to open in the next few years.

Cycling

Travelling by bike might not be the first choice for everyone in heavy rain, but if it's only a light shower, then cycling remains a good option. Bear in mind Edinburgh is a city built on seven hills – the ones you're most likely to encounter are Arthur's Seat, Castle Rock,

Calton Hill and Blackford Hill – and the topography means you're always going up or down somewhere when you're in the saddle. For bike hire, the following companies are recommended: Cycle Scotland (Blackfriars Street, off the Royal Mile), Leith Cycle Co. (Leith Walk) and Zoomo e-bikes (Hanover Street; for week-long rentals only). Commonly, all rental bikes have lights and mudguards, but in Edinburgh wide tyres and good brakes are recommended because of the city's cobblestoned streets and tram lines. You might also want a waterproof, for obvious reasons.

Taxis

Edinburgh's streets are home to two different sorts of taxi – signature black cabs and mini cabs. There are two black cab companies – City Cabs and Central Taxis – and you can hail either on the street, find one at a designated taxi rank or pre-book one through their respective app. It's often quicker (and far more comfortable) to order a taxi on your device from the comfort of a restaurant or bar, rather than waiting on the street in the rain for one to turn up. Black cabs are usually the most expensive taxi option – they are metered and come with a minimum starting fee. For a mini cab, there are several companies and most of these need to be booked online in advance. Alternatively, there's also a wealth of taxi apps – Uber is by far the most popular and reliable one to use in the city.

Central

Mind-boggling is the phrase mostly associated with Edinburgh's Old Town. It's a pop-up storybook brought to life and layered with cobblestone wynds, gothic churches, cannon-topped crags, and wonky tolbooths providing a sublime backdrop for cultural and historical adventures that are the envy of the rest of the world. There's far more to central Edinburgh than scene-stealing steeples and acropolis-topped Calton Hill though, and this easily-navigable cluster of streets is where you'll find many of Scotland's liveliest restaurants and smart shops, as well as museums and pubs almost purpose-built for rainy days and romantic nights. The theatrical Royal Mile is known for its time-warp appeal, while below the bridges in the medieval underbelly of the Old Town you'll find the Grassmarket and Cowgate, where here-and-now pubs and restaurants segue into nightclubs and cocktail bars.

The Lookout by Gardener's Cottage

The views from the top of Calton Hill – home to a fine collection of a neo-classical monument, a fluted-column memorial and a trophy watchtower – cause a stir on Instagram, but those from this restaurant perch within the City Observatory walls aren't just pretty. While filling your retinas with the skyline's walloping spires and steeples, the other rewards are some of Edinburgh's most memorable cuisine and dropping the needle on a scene-setting LP from the open-access vinyl record collection beside the kitchen. Come for a tasting menu lunch or dinner, and find utter joy in a menu that's rich in local produce. In just a few dishes – Perthshire mallard, Shetland hake, Dunbar crab, and Lanarkshire cheese with Edinburgh honey – you've covered the four points of the compass.

38 Calton Hill, EH7 5AA
thelookoutedinburgh.co
@thelookoutbygc

The Witchery

The Witchery

Look for the distinctive stone townhouse at the top of the Royal Mile, then peer through the windows looking down to this dimly-lit subterranean restaurant, and you'll find a slice of 18th-century Edinburgh transported to today. The decor – flickering candelabras, tasseled curtains, marble busts – wouldn't look out of place in a novel like *Dracula* or *Frankenstein* and the vibe is Gothic love nest with a hint of make-believe. Of the menus, there's a two-course lunch by candlelight and afternoon tea on offer, but it's the à la carte evening one that ranks amongst the capital's most spectacular. Fittingly, dishes are characterized by the sort you'd find at a royal banquet, so expect the likes of roast guinea fowl, lemon sole and Scotch beef fillet as bloody as you like it. For a complete showstopper, try the Balmoral Estate Roe Deer Wellington – as traditional as it is terrific.

352 Castlehill, EH1 2NF
thewitchery.com
@the.witchery
🏛

Mother India's Cafe

Glasgow, not Edinburgh, is technically the curry capital of Scotland, but that doesn't stop this hotspot of Punjabi spice and dead-ringer for the faded splendour of Mumbai's Irani cafes, and it packs out every night and weekend. The holy grail here is Indian small plates, of the sort you don't really want to share, and all served on tables soundtracked by irrepressible chatter. From the pages of the menu, you'll spy classics (dosas, samosas, biryanis and nostril-tingling Butter Chicken), but top choices are those that require a little extra legwork in the kitchen, like Monkfish Tikka, Spiced Haddock and the signature Curried Lamb with Poppy Seeds and Cream. As curry and lager marry together like Scots and good times, pop in to The Royal Oak next door afterwards to hear a fiddle session at the legendary folk music pub.

3–5 Infirmary Street, EH1 1LT
motherindia.co.uk
@officialmotherindia
🏛 ☺

Timberyard

This rewarding converted warehouse restaurant was made for theatrical lunches and dinner – in a previous life it was used as a props and costume store. From the double-height ceiling to the pillars, blackboards and dangly light fittings, Timberyard is pared-back, yet puts you at ease with a wood-burner and wool blankets, and staff who know exactly how to make you feel that you're not just here to make up the numbers. So they'll encourage you to relax and graze with a bite and beverage before settling in for the main event (a grand four-course lunch or seven-course tasting menu with paired wines). Sipping a cider or French wine, you'll move onto dishes that focus on one chief ingredient (pheasant, scallop, turbot, delica pumpkin, for instance), but marry the fine arts of pickling and foraging with curing and smoking. A moody dish like Smoked Eel, King Cabbage and Quince says it all.

10 Lady Lawson Street, EH3 9DS
timberyard.co
@timberyard10
🗏 ☺

The Milkman

This gorgeous speciality coffee shop sheds light on the past of one of the Old Town's most colourful streets. The building first opened in 1898, back in the days of horse-drawn carts and gas lamps, and though the coffee baristas took tenant-ship of the address in 2015 the essence is still very much of nostalgia – it was once an old sweetshop and the stone walls, windlasses for the shutters and stone-tiled floor are imbued with memories and as authentic as they come. From the bespoke 150-year-old reclaimed wooden counter, you'll pick a window bench seat with a Fair Trade espresso and peanut butter cookie or gluten-free carrot cake, then sit back to watch the city rush past you, with collars upturned and umbrellas blown inside out. To delve deeper into The Milkman story, pop across the cobblestones to the top of the street to the sibling coffeehouse at number 52.

7 Cockburn Street, EH1 1BP
Other location: Old Town (same street)
themilkman.coffee
@themilkmancoffee

The Bow Bar

For those who love no-nonsense, no-frills drinking establishments, this pub on much-photographed Victoria Street is a place where you know exactly what you're getting: cask ales, top-shelf single malt whiskies and good-natured social banter from in-the-know locals. The out-of-time layout and stripped-back atmosphere – no food, no music, no TVs, slimline wooden tables only large enough to sit a pint or dram – never fail to impress visitors, even if many fail to make it past the swing doors. Once inside, though, the knowledgeable staff are connoisseurs of their craft, and can help talk you through more than 400 whiskies, plus rotating guest kegs and casks, sours, IPAs, blondes, stouts, porters, lambics and lagers. Cosy to a point, it's little wonder there's often a curled-up Collie, Pug or Scottish Terrier sat beneath the bar.

80 W Bow, EH1 2HH
thebowbar.co.uk
@the_bow_bar_edinburgh

The Devil's Advocate

One of the joys of this inviting pub-kitchen hybrid is finding it. Almost in the belly of the city, off the Royal Mile and out of sight on one of the Old Town's crooked, sunshine-starved closes, it's known for its seasonal Scottish food and carousel of single malts stacked up against centuries-old stone. The menu for the mezzanine dining area changes, but there are favourites that never fall from grace – like the Smoked Fish Platter, Slow-cook Pork Belly, Rosemary Lamb Shank and Spiced Roasted Cauliflower. Location-wise, you're actually in the relic of a Victorian pump house, with lofty ceiling and post-industrial chic ventilation ducts, but away from this history, the bar area has the air of here-and-now: house cocktails are exercises in tinkering with taste (not many bartenders would mix peaty Laphroaig whisky with Banane du Brésil liquor). Should you fall for the overall vibe, owner The Bon Vivant Group runs all-day diner Luckenbooths around the cobblestoned corner.

9 Advocate's Close, EH1 1ND
devilsadvocateedinburgh.co.uk
@TheDAOldTown

Sandy Bell's

Sandy Bell's

There are few better spent fivers than that on a pint at this dark, wooden-walled pub, which has been putting on lively folk sessions since 1942. At the right time of day, with the fire blazing, whisky roaring and musicians tuning up, it is as if time has stopped outside and you've stepped behind a magic curtain into a world of half-drunken folklorists and guitar pickers. Everyone who's anyone in the Scottish folk music scene has played or sang here – the roll call includes The Corries (who wrote *Flower of Scotland*), Gerry Rafferty, Sir Billy Connolly, Dougie MacLean, Barbara Dickson and Bert Jansch, a major influence on Neil Young and Led Zeppelin – but you needn't be an aficionado to feel at home. Simply grab a drink and a seat by the fire as a Scots or Irish music session sparks to life, and you've got a boozer worth travel bragging about.

25 Forrest Road, EH1 2QH
sandybells.com

Café Royal

The word ornate does not do this 19th-century drinking saloon justice. Walls are hung with ceramic murals and gilded mirrors, and the rest is a rich marriage of stained glass windows, chandelier lights, gold cornicing and Victorian plasterwork. To Edinburgh residents, it's far from a typical boozer – it opened in 1826 as Scotland's first oyster and champagne house – and is now a listed building, with more than a whiff of nostalgia. Fittingly, the pub serves a well-heeled clientele, with its off Princes Street location also a lure for savvy visitors, and the food menu reflects the opulent surroundings. In a city full of fish-and-chips shops, the bar is raised here with iced towers of lobster, Atlantic prawns and potted brown shrimp, plus there are mussels and Loch Fyne rock oysters from the west coast. The seafood (and steaks) might hog the limelight, but for less rich thrills, this remains an out-and-out destination for guzzling and gossiping – just like the original patrons did nearly 200 years ago.

19 West Register Street, EH2 2AA
caferoyaledinburgh.com
@CafeRoyalEDN

Lilith's Lounge (aka House of Gods cocktail bar)

Something wicked this way comes: the House of Gods is a rock star hotel in the Cowgate that works best as a buzzy place to escape the weather, with a decadent late-night cocktail bar that has a Garden of Eden theme and more than a touch of the divine. Unblighted by the tourist crowds, secretive Lilith's Lounge has darkly dramatic interiors, from twisted cobra stem lamps to animal hide prints and jungle ferns, and a backstory inspired by that of Lilith, the primordial Queen of the Damned and alternative first wife of Adam. It's great fun as a couple or with a crowd, with a tarot-themed cocktail menu and – get this – a licence to serve all sorts of midnight garden inspired libations until 3am.

233 Cowgate, EH1 1JQ
houseofgodshotel.com
@houseofgodshotel

National Museum
of Scotland

The joy of visiting Edinburgh's largest free museum is it's the most memorable place to tumble through time on a journey from Scotland's prehistory to modern times. That means this labyrinth-like collection of themed galleries is a treasure trove of curated trinkets, natural history wonders and stand-out exhibits that reflect on anthropology, Scottish history and the country's scientific contributions to the world. Start seeking out items like Bonnie Prince Charlie's picnic set and the distinctive medieval Lewis chessmen, as born to life at the climax of *Harry Potter and the Philosopher's Stone*, or find your way to Dolly, the first cloned mammal and the most famous sheep in the world. Other objects of veneration include the Millennium clock, which captivates and terrifies little ones in equal measure thanks to its hourly display of moving skulls and kinetic statues, a giant T-Rex skeleton and the oldest surviving colour TV. You could spend a week inside the galleries, but should you find it all too much, plot a route to the second floor café for a breather in the light-filled Grand Gallery atrium.

Chambers Street, EH1 1JF
nms.ac.uk
@nationalmuseumsscotland
☺ ✪

Dovecot Studios

Dovecot Studios

This working tapestry studio and landmark design centre has more than 110 years of history and was first based in the western suburb of Corstorphine before moving into this former public swimming pool. That gives it a well-lit, graceful vibe and it's a thrill to walk around the multi-coloured hangar and see craftspeople and master weavers bring works of art to life before your eyes from the first-floor viewing balcony (check the opening times before you visit). You can browse and linger in the gallery, café and shop, while there are tapestries and rugs to liven up your own house or apartment and – time your visit wisely – and you'll be able to join a rug tufting or life drawing class, embroidery or bookbinding workshop, or hands-on, fleece-to-fabric experience with one of the looms.

10 Infirmary Street, EH1 1LT
dovecotstudios.com
@dovecotstudios
☺ ✩

The Writers' Museum

Whether you're a bookworm or just getting to grips with the disproportionate influence of Edinburgh writers on the world of literature (J.K. Rowling, Irvine Welsh, Ian Rankin, Sir Arthur Conan Doyle, Muriel Spark to name a few), a visit to this free museum off the Royal Mile is worth a few hours of your time. For context, the city was the first to be named a UNESCO City of Literature and the museum is a tribute to three colossi of the art that have long left critics flailing for superlatives: Scotland's national bard Robert Burns, *Rob Roy* and *Ivanhoe* author Sir Walter Scott, and *Treasure Island* and *The Strange Case of Dr Jekyll and Mr Hyde* wordsmith Robert Louis Stevenson. Inside, you'll see first editions, inkwells, portraits, personal effects, a printing press and Burns' writing desk. Outside, meanwhile, on Makars' Court, you'll find the Edinburgh equivalent of the Hollywood Walk of Fame: a space of inscribed flagstones that celebrate a who's who of Scottish writers.

Lawnmarket, Lady Stair's Close, EH1 2PA
edinburghmuseums.org.uk
@museumsgalleriesedinburgh
☺ ✩

Camera Obscura & World of Illusions

In many ways, Edinburgh is a city built on the principles of science and its oldest attraction (in business since 1853) is this multi-storey tenement tower of optical illusions, interactive puzzles and mind tricks. Add in a rooftop with stellar views of the city and the historic camera obscura itself – a pre-cinema dark chamber that reflects and projects live images onto a table – and you have a recipe for a corker of a day out, especially if you have kids in tow. It's also the sort of place that packs out on a rainy day: it's open late (and even later at weekends – see the website for details), so plan your visit first thing or around sunset for divine, sky-stroked views of the Old Town from the roof.

549 Castlehill, Royal Mile, EH1 2ND
camera-obscura.co.uk
@camobscura1
☺

City Art Centre

Waverley Station is crowded and chaotic, so this art gallery across the street is a balm, whatever the weather. It's set in a striking building with a storied history, having been home to both *The Scotsman* newspaper office and the city's wholesale fruit and vegetable market. The outside is all about classic elegance – it was envisioned as an iron-framed warehouse and the facade is tempered by Parisian Beaux-Arts architecture – while inside the galleries are split across six floors where you can dig into historic and contemporary Scottish arts. The immersive collection encompasses more than 4,500 items, meaning the prints, photographs, sculptures and paintings change regularly and you're unlikely to scratch the surface with what's on display. Despite its Old Town location, the galleries lend themselves perfectly to peaceful contemplation and there's a Mimi's Bakehouse for coffee and cake culture on the ground floor.

2 Market Street, EH1 1DE
edinburghmuseums.org
@museumsgalleriesedinburgh
☺ ⭐

The Red Door Gallery

The rooms of your house or flat might feel second-best if you visit this superlative print showroom in the heart of the Old Town and leave empty-handed. The art captures the character of the city and Scotland through sketches, colourful maps and lithographs, and there's as much an emphasis on landscape and street scenes as there is anthropomorphic Highland cows and cats. Even if your home doesn't need a spruce up, it's still worth a snoop to see the showcase of work from more than 150 artists and creatives. And for that small takeaway souvenir, there's an elegant selection of artist cards, enamel pins, jewellery and plenty of gifts under £10.

42 Victoria Street, EH1 2JW
edinburghart.com
@reddoor_gallery

Avalanche Records

Allow plenty of time and space in your backpack or luggage for the treats and rarities at this shopping-mall set independent and alternative record store next to Waverley Station that's been keeping Edinburgh locals dancing, rocking and raving for the past four decades. Owner Kevin Buckle knows his stock and is a godfather of the local music scene, with opinion columns appearing weekly in the local newspaper, and if you're a pop magpie then he might well talk you into buying a rare pressing or limited edition blue vinyl. Otherwise, step in to warm up and dry off, browse the rock-band T-shirts and exclusive cult pop art pieces from Brazilian artist Butcher Billy, then have a look around the other flurry of vendors.

Waverley Mall, EH1 1BQ
avalancherecords.co.uk
@avalanche_edin

Cadenhead's Whisky Shop

Cadenhead's Whisky Shop

With such unrivalled whisky heritage across Scotland, it should come as no surprise that distillers and bottlers lay down all sorts of claims about their history. Some need a stiff dram to take seriously, but this is Scotland's oldest independent bottler, in business since 1842, and though its origins lie in Campbeltown on the Kintyre peninsula, it is one of Edinburgh's longest running retailers. Inside, it's part old-school apothecary, part whisky library and is a cultured setting for picking up a rare bottle of single malt Scotch or for a whisky tasting – the peaty aroma of the whisky can almost be felt in the warp and weft of the place. You'll love it because – oddly enough – all the other tourists stick to the other, more commercial whisky-selling boutiques closer to The Scotch Whisky Experience farther up the Royal Mile.

172 Canongate, EH8 8DF
cadenhead.shop
@wmcadenheads

W. Armstrong & Son

A top-hatted circus ringmaster, a Moulin Rouge burlesque dancer, a Biggles-era fighter pilot: as you walk into this vintage clothing emporium it's impossible not to imagine how your life might have played out as someone else entirely. If you like the idea of dressing up or adding some one-of-a-kind clothing to your wardrobe, then this thrift store is a sexy Shangri-La that's brimful of fun fashion ideas. Tumble back through time and try on 1960s-era Mod gear or 1970s bohemian wear to gear you up for next year's music festivals, or go grunge, graphic or whatever takes your fancy. There are three other branches, so if you don't find the exact colour of feather boa that you're looking for, the fashion-forward staff can help direct you to the store that can best influence your new look. Otherwise, with it raining outside, a waterproof Mackintosh coat should work wonders.

Craigs Close, 29 Cockburn Street, EH1 1BN
Other locations: Grassmarket, Old Town, Newington
@armstrongs_vintage_edinburgh

I.J. Mellis

Take an appetite-piquing stroll down pastel-coloured Victoria Street and you'll find it hard to not cross the threshold of this legendary Aladdin's cave. The first sight through the storefront window is of huge wheels of farmhouse cheddars, stiltons and camemberts, blues and bries, and the pickings are just as rich when nosing around inside: witness rare Scottish cow, goat and sheep cheeses like tomme-style Laganory, creamy Isle of Mull Cheddar and slightly boozy Hebridean Blue, plus hanging saucissons and shelves stacked with oils, quinces, figgy jams and condiments. The design is all raw brickwork and floor tiles with a cluster of vintage milk churns for good measure, while queues often snake out onto the street. Opened in 1993, founder Iain and his son Rory Mellis now run a cheese empire, with stores elsewhere in Edinburgh (including a wine and cheese bar at the back of its gentrified Morningside cheesemonger), as well as in Glasgow and St Andrews.

30 Victoria Street, EH1 2JW
Other locations: Stockbridge, Morningside
mellischeese.net
@mellischeeseltd

North

The world's first example of a planned, grid-layout urban area (take that, Manhattan), the glorious New Town is the heart and soul of north Edinburgh. It's chock-a-block with rows of Georgian-era houses and private gardens, but also where locals escape the city centre to linger in cafés, pubs and restaurants. The neighbourhood celebrates good times as much as it does architecture and art, and this part of town then leads to chi-chi Stockbridge, where independent boutiques and wine bars couple up on much-heralded streets that are both bonnie and brimming with character. Beyond here, the shoreline of the Firth of Forth beckons, along with a storied castle that's full of antiquity and pomp.

The Scran & Scallie

Back in 2013, there really was no such thing as a gastro-pub in the city; nowhere that served Michelin-star class cuisine along with a crisp pint, or a grand Sunday lunch for the family with carefully-chosen wines. How chefs Tom Kitchin and Dominic Jack changed all that. Nowadays, this neighbourhood haunt is a prime city go-to (reservations are almost always necessary) and it'll only be a matter of time before you're part of its fan club. The deal is a laidback family-friendly affair, with down-to-earth classics like fish pie, seasonal game and a steak pie with a marrow bone top hat. Despite the higher-end prices, it's far from snooty, with a pared-back design that looks like a snuggly Scandi-meets-Stockbridge pub – cue stag antlers, charcoal-smeared walls and crackling stove. On the menu, too, is a slap-up selection of heartstring-plucking puddings: a sticky toffee cake paired with a caramel whisky dram is the fuel you'll need to drag yourself back out into the streets.

1 Comely Bank Road, Stockbridge, EH4 1DR
scranandscallie.com
@scranandscallie
🏢 ☺

Café St Honoré

Café St Honoré

At some point while exploring Edinburgh's New Town you'll find yourself on Thistle Street. It's home to bumper-to-bumper restaurants and popular pubs, but only those in the know duck into this delightful Scottish-French brasserie on a dog-leg lane off the main street. This is a textbook Gallic affair, with frilly curtains, large white tablecloths, bulging wine racks and all manner of hat tips to the auld alliance between the two countries. For instance, just when you thought you knew all there was to know about honest French cooking, then you come across a dish like Confit Duck Leg with Stornoway Black Pudding, or Pear and Endive Salad with Lanark Blue Cheese – the hearty Scottish ingredients are always brought to the fore. Otherwise, you're here for the neighbourhood feel and warm service and to meet chef director Neil Forbes, a stalwart of the Edinburgh gourmet scene.

34 North West Thistle Street Lane,
EH2 1EA
cafesthonore.com
@cafesthonore
🗓

Noto

Chef-owner Stuart Ralton is a staple of the local food landscape, with two other raved-about restaurants in the city: fine dining Aizle on Charlotte Square in the West End and pasta go-to Tipo on Hanover Street. But it is this small-plates specialist, inspired by the boss' time working in New York and his love for Japan, that's made for rainy days and picking over the inspiring food and drink menus. Toss up between the North Sea Crab with Warm Butter or Beef Tartare with Jerusalem Artichoke, then it's on to Miso Cod, Borders Short Rib or Chicken Yakitori (and yes, there are great vegetarian and vegan options like Aubergine Tonkatsu and Broccoli Tempura). With an overtly minimalist look (an uncluttered bar, an almost monotone colour scheme, a tokenistic climbing plant), there's little to distract you from the food on offer. Which is great really, because it's absolutely terrific.

47A Thistle Street, EH2 1DY
notoedinburgh.co.uk
@notoedinburgh
🗓

Artisan Roast

In the beginning was coffee. At least that's how it feels these days, with baristas and cafés on every corner – but this Edinburgh-wide establishment got there first. It has the distinction of being Edinburgh's first speciality roastery, opening in 2007 on Broughton Street in Leith, but this cosy-chic Stockbridge satellite is serious business for Fair Trade coffee drinking, people watching and daytime dawdling. Coming here feels like part of the daily routine for many locals, with single-origin bean hand-brewed coffees always swooningly delicious. There's more to the café than beans and blends though: breakfast, lunch and cake are also on the menu, while baristas sell hand-crafted cups, equipment and masterclasses (as well as pouches filled with coffee flavour experiments). If the pale sun is shining, take a table on the street; otherwise, squeeze up beside the mish-mash of patrons hunkered inside.

100A Raeburn Place, Stockbridge, EH4 1HH
Other locations: New Town, Brunstfield, Leith
artisanroast.co.uk
@artisanroastcoffeeroasters
☺

Fortitude Coffee

Here's a New Town coffee shop that doesn't take itself too seriously. It now has two other branches, but this low-key and compact nook next to The Stand Comedy Club (see page 46) is the capital's most accessible setting for its single origin coffees, cinnamon swirls and light bites. A sign of its success is the brand has branched out from just its own house-roasted beans to kombuchas, flavoured caramels and more, and the minimalist café is now as much an aficionado's barista boutique as it is a place for a quick cup of joe on one of the stools. To give it a final quirky touch, clipboard menus dangle from the wall, each detailing the just-roast coffees available during your visit.

3C York Place, EH1 3EB
Other locations: Stockbridge, Newington
fortitudecoffee.com
@fortitudecoffee

St Vincent Bar

If you could peer through the subterranean stained glass windows of this Georgian-era townhouse, the blissed-out faces would say it all: this is an old-school pub, with an emphasis on community and old-fashioned hospitality. As simple briefs go, it fits it perfectly, so this is the kind of place you could lose hours, chatting to new friends, nursing a pint of cask ale or glass of wine, or fussing over the dogs that can be regularly found on the floor at their owners' feet. There's cheese, charcuterie and pretzels for a reboot if you're hungry, plus a sizeable record collection for a groovy soundtrack, pub quizzes and a dog 'wall of fame'. 'The Vinnie', as adoring locals call it, also shows crucial football and rugby games. For a similarly hip vibe, check out Nightcap, the pub's sister cocktail bar on York Place, just off Queen Street.

11 St Vincent Street, Stockbridge, EH3 6SW
stvincentbar.com
@stvincentbar

The Last Word Saloon

Imitation speakeasies were all the rage a few years ago and there's no better place in Edinburgh to ferret away with an Old Fashioned or this cocktail bar's prohibition-era signature drink, a Last Word – for the uninitiated, that's a ballsy muddle of gin, green Chartreuse, maraschino and lime. The strict Thursday to Monday opening times give the downstairs basement saloon the air of a dirty little secret and the vibe is of a dimly-lit snug, with roaring fire, Chesterfield armchairs and barrel seating. Clued-in drinkers know the drill – reservations are pretty important here – and for those who prefer their drink without a salted grapefruit soda or matcha green tea mixer, there are several fine newfangled Scottish beers to try: namely, Newbarns Pilsner and Pilot IPA.

44 St Stephen Street, Stockbridge, EH3 5AL
lastwordsaloon.com
@lastwordsaloon

The Lucky Liquor Co.

The Lucky Liquor Co.

Queen Street, caught between a strip of off-limits private residential gardens and the well-heeled boutiques of George Street, is often overlooked as a destination to eat, drink and hang out. Strolling from west to east though, you might notice a few hidden-in-plain-sight cocktail bars that scream party time. There's Panda & Sons (supposedly a street-level barber shop) and, farther along, Bramble, tucked down an understated staircase that's easy to miss. Run by the same team nearby is The Lucky Liquor Co. and its oddball pitch is 13 experimental, if euphoric, cocktails made from 13 different spirits that change every 13 weeks. With limited opening hours, you'll want to reserve a table to dig into tipples like Disco Pisco (El Gobernador Pisco, blue Curacao, lime, egg white) and Buns 'n' Roses (whisky, cinnamon bun tea, Madeira). To take a slice of The Lucky Liquor Co. home with you, parent company Mothership sells all sorts of cocktail sets, spirits and fruit sodas too.

39A Queen Street, New Town, EH2 3NH
luckyliquorco.com
@luckyliquorco

Good Brothers Wine Bar

Winos of the world unite! This Stockbridge wine salon, away from the bustle of popular neighbourhood pubs Hectors and The Stockbridge Tap, asserts the belief in the virtues of sustainable wine and viticulture and is of the greatest interest to anyone who likes to learn the origins of their drink. The bar is run by brothers Graeme and Rory Sutherland and does its best to mimic an Italian enoteca, with bar bites along the lines of sardines, anchovies, cheese boards and charcuterie, and tables for groups as well as counter seating. Chat to the staff and they'll likely recommend a Pinot Noir, Chardonnay, Riesling or Nebbiolo with a hint of bias – they're all the owners' favourite grape appellations. Should you get stuck in the rain on the western fringe of the city, then the brothers also run Little Rascal bottle shop and bar in Corstorphine.

4–6 Dean Street, Stockbridge, EH4 1LW
goodbrothers.co.uk
@GoodBrosWine

The Cumberland Bar

Rain or shine, the slow tick of time is a licence to drink from one of the real ale taps or linger over lunch at this classic establishment squirrelled away in a part of the New Town that many visitors never reach. If it sounds familiar, that's because it has a starring role in Edinburgh-based author Alexander McCall Smith's serialized novel *44 Scotland Street*, but nonetheless this is a pub for book lovers or not. There's plenty of brass taps and polished woodwork, a radiant testament to the fact that alcohol has been served on the premises in various guises since 1832, and the tiered beer garden is for rejoicing when it's warm enough to sit outside for drunken late-night conversations. For two other classic pubs under the same ownership, visit The Guildford Arms or The Abbotsford Bar & Restaurant – both of which are on or near the city's pedestrianized pub thoroughfare Rose Street.

1–3 Cumberland Street, New Town, EH3 6RT
cumberlandbar.co.uk
@Cumberland7

Scottish National Portrait Gallery

Steps away from one of Edinburgh's most heavily-trafficked thoroughfares lies this formidable neo-gothic memory-palace, where you'll find paintings and photo tributes that tell the story of Scotland's heroes and heroines. The red sandstone gallery is one of the most beautiful in the country, with all eyes awed by the Great Hall, a tour-de-force of an introduction centred around a beyond-spectacular gallery and first-floor ornamental parapet, where you can view a processional frieze showing more than 150 titans of Scottish history. Besides all the familiar faces – from Mary, Queen of Scots to The Proclaimers – the hallowed art hall is a benchmark setter – it opened in 1889 as the world's first purpose-built portrait gallery. Between paying respects to the paintings, sate yourself with lunch or coffee and cake at Café Portrait, the gallery's veg-friendly bistro for a slap-up salad, sandwich or quiche.

1 Queen Street, EH2 1JD
nationalgalleries.org
@natgalleriessco
☺ ✿

Inverleith House

Georgian down to its very bones, with majestic stone walls, turret-style spire and a former Scottish baronet owner, this former mansion house doubles as a centrepiece of the Royal Botanic Gardens and much-used exhibition space. Before becoming enveloped fully into the sprawling constellation of plants, trees and shrubs, the manor was home to the Scottish National Gallery of Modern Art, but now it's been reimagined as 'Climate House'. On a wet day, you can slip inside to learn more about the three-year project, which aims to highlight the climate emergency – and to change the way the world views the biodiversity crisis – through artist-led exhibitions.

Royal Botanic Garden, Inverleith Row, EH3 5LR
rbge.org.uk
@rbgecreative
☺ ✪

The Stand Comedy Club

Laughter spilling onto the streets is a permanent soundtrack in Edinburgh: this is the home of the world-renowned Fringe Festival after all, and each August the city puts on more than 1,100-odd comedy shows. Many of those acts, from up-and-coming newcomers to award-winning TV show headliners, have taken to the intimate basement stage here and because the trailblazing club is Scotland's original purpose-built comedy venue, expect tour-de-force performers on at any time of the day, not only at night. Long-time cult comedian and Edinburgh regular Stewart Lee even describes the venue as 'arguably the world's most perfect stand-up room'. Indeed, stop by yourself and you'll also discover that this is a place stirred by pleasure all year round.

5 York Place, EH1 3EB
thestand.co.uk
@standcomedyclub
🏛

The Stand Comedy Club

The Scottish Gallery

In the heart of the New Town – a couple of blocks from the city centre, a couple more from well-groomed Stockbridge – this sleek contemporary art gallery is on a stretch of road well-populated by art dealers and rival gallerists. But contemplating the art from its Georgian townhouse, you know you've come to the right place, as there are rooms full of stunning landscapes, portraits and ceramics. The programme takes its lead from who's up-and-coming on the Scottish contemporary art scene and is as much a place to appreciate creativity as it is to pop in to enjoy a revolving door's worth of artist talks, book launches and touring exhibitions from named artists. Got a real passion for art? The Dundas Street Gallery next door also hosts regular exhibitions, while Greyfriars Art two doors down is one of the city's leading art materials suppliers.

16 Dundas Street, EH3 6HZ
scottish-gallery.co.uk
@scottishgallery
☺ ✪

Lauriston Castle

A little known fact about Scotland's capital city: it has three castles, not just the one as most people think. There's marquee Edinburgh Castle atop the Royal Mile in the Old Town; imposing Craigmillar Castle, once a safe haven for Mary, Queen of Scots and brimming with nooks and crannies three miles to the southeast of the city; and this supposedly haunted 16th-century tower house four miles to the northwest, which is arguably the pick of the bunch. When it's raining, you can take bus #41 from Princes Street to the shoreline woods and Japanese garden and into the heart of the castle, but access is by pre-booked weekend tour only (there's a family tour option too, see the website for times). Inside, you'll discover museum-piece interiors that epitomized the Scottish Edwardian era and among the thousands of items curated by the former well-travelled owners are Eastern rugs, fine examples of Parisian furniture, table tops and writing desks from Naples, Sicily, Venice and Rome. Warm up afterwards with coffee and cake from family-run Mimi's Bakehouse within the castle grounds.

2 Cramond Road South, EH4 6AD
edinburghmuseums.org.uk
@museumsgalleriesedinburgh
🏛 ☺

An Independent Zebra

This homewares and gift store is a Xanadu of delightful finds and is packed with cushions and lampshades, framed wall art, books, mugs, candles and cards all hoarded like riches, with hats, gloves and scarves for good measure. Squeeze between the display stands and hovering locals – there's so much on sale there's little room to move at times between the shelves and larger items of furniture – then dare yourself to leave empty handed. Fittingly for a popular place in trend-setting Stockbridge, most of the items are the creations of Scottish-based independent designers, craft makers and up-cyclers, underlining how important supporting grassroots creative industries is to the owner and staff.

88–92 Raeburn Place, Stockbridge, EH4 1HH
anindependentzebra.com
@indiezeb

VoxBox Music

With the front of this shop crammed with crates of vinyl and its back room a library of thousands of half-forgotten LPs and singles, there are few places more suited to record hunters in Edinburgh than this Stockbridge labour of love. Owner Darren's passion for pop (and blues, jazz, rock, reggae, you name it) is at the heart of it all and, with the major upswing in vinyl releases, there are as many new releases from local independent labels to get excited about. Give your second-hand pick a spin on its 1960s Dansette record, or keep things quiet so as not to disturb the in-store live specials or open mic sessions which happen regularly.

21 St Stephen Street, Stockbridge, EH3 5AN
voxboxmusic.co.uk
@voxboxmusic

Homer

The New Town was residential first, trendy second. And sitting pretty at the centre of its Venn diagram is this homeware and lifestyle brand. It first sparked to life in Aberfeldy, Perthshire, before coming to take over a townhouse in the capital and is now a den of Scot-Scandi and status-symbol furniture upholstered in tweeds and Georgian-era rooms, broadly themed around the living room, library, kitchen, bedroom and shed. Within each, you'll find that perfect something for that difficult space at home, be it a hardwood bureau, totem hall stand, floor lamp, mango wood stool or reclaimed cubbyhole unit. And should you be visiting a local resident, this is where many also get the Nordic ceramics, tartan throws, sheepskins and candles that liven up their living spaces – fret not, delivery can be arranged no matter where you stay.

8 Howe Street, EH3 6TD
athomer.co.uk
@homeredinburgh

Homer

Golden Hare Books

How many bookshops are cosy enough to have a wood-burning stove fireplace set in-between the packed shelves of paperbacks and novels? Golden Hare Books is such a find and one that makes a perfect place to dry out in the company of a fine book – the specialities here are independent-published titles and carefully-curated fiction and non-fiction tomes from the book-crazed staff; as the saying here goes, 'all our books are important'. In business since 2012, it remains a thrill to seek out your new favourite while sheltering from the rain – though with more than 2,000 titles from travel to cookery to science-fiction to kids' picture books, you might be here longer than you think. Also impressive is the calendar of events, which runs the spectrum from author talks and book signings to workshops and book clubs.

68 St Stephen Street, Stockbridge, EH3 5AQ
goldenharebooks.com
@goldenharebooks
☺

treen

As brand slogans go, treen's is an absolute zinger. 'A killer wardrobe without killing the planet' is the tag and this vegan lifestyle fashion brand works closely with producers to make a positive difference, shifting the conversation away from fast to slow fashion – have you ever considered wearing apple waste as a leather alternative, for instance? So, if you're on a hunt for your next favourite item of clothing, or considering switching your lifestyle with an entire wardrobe makeover, owner Cat Anderson is the Stockbridge fashion guru to get advice from. On the racks, there's a focus on both womenswear and men's, with jackets and coats, shirts and dresses, trousers and denims, but also plenty of cruelty-free skincare sets, candles, perfumes and body oils. Undoubtedly, the world needs more retailers like this.

2–4 St Stephen Place, Stockbridge, EH3 5AJ
shoptreen.com
@shoptreen_

West

All the drama of modern Edinburgh is on display
in the west of the city and there's no shortage of
memorable cafés and restaurants, brilliant pubs
and must-visit shops. Most journeys start west of
Princes Street in the West End, where landmark
William Street lays claim to being the coolest
place to shop and pub hop in the whole city.
Busier, if farther west, is Haymarket,
a rejuvenated cluster of streets focused around
the train station and tram hub, and to the
southwest is up-and-coming Fountainbridge
on the Union Canal.

BABA

Mopping up plates with freshly-torn pita is an art form at this Levant-inspired bistro restaurant with kitchen aromas and sharp-flavoured signatures fit for an Ottoman sultan. Consider the Venison Carpaccio topped with Whipped Feta, or Hot-smoked Sea Trout with Burnt Lemon Yoghurt, compulsory as a far-from-ordinary mezze starter, then it's on to a main course of Charcoal Grilled Chuck-eye Steak, Sea Bass or Spiced Broccoli with all the trimmings. All meals come with sparkling service and mood-setting Eastern Mediterranean cocktails – hibiscus, mint and pomegranate are served up here like they're going out of fashion – and the flavours of Lebanon, Syria and Yemen are complemented by a look that is a mash-up of a Moroccan carpet bazaar and posing Beiruti cocktail joint. It works though, as does the location, which tethers the restaurant to the ground-floor lobby of the Kimpton Charlotte Square hotel next door.

130 George Street, EH2 4JZ
baba.restaurant
@babaedinburgh
🏢 ☺

The Palmerston

If you're caught between Princes Street and Haymarket in a downpour, then this restaurant and café is a terrific destination to run for cover. Once home to a bank, then a low-key coffee shop, the corner site has been revamped into a polished wood and partially-tiled destination for trendy nosh (with a lot of focus on its daily tasting menu). The sense is the Australian-Scots owners love the detail in land and sea dining and are firm friends with local farmers and fishermen. So you could get Crispy Pig's Head or Pickled Tripe Salad or Tagliatelle with Salt Cod and Artichokes, but you might not: the menu changes that fast. The measure of its main courses, though, is that you can expect hearty dishes, such as Hogged Fagott, Ox's Liver or Fish Stew. The other showstopper here is the on-site bakery, which supplies breads to other cafés and restaurants throughout the city – so try the exquisite grub, or come before lunch for equally heart-filling coffee and pastries.

1 Palmerston Place, EH12 5AF
thepalmerstonedinburgh.co.uk
@the_palmerston
🏛

Ting Thai Caravan

Co-owners Ting and Ae Tapparat first sparked up their street-stall woks at the Edinburgh Fringe Festival more than a decade ago and their story is one of hot spice and hard-working success. Now, the duo and their army of Thai chefs have two restaurants – one overlooking Potterrow beside the University of Edinburgh and this perennially busy bistro that draws locals by the tuk-tuk load. Specialities to whet your appetite include *Nua Yam Talay* (rump steak with spicy lime, coriander and chilli glaze), Seabass *Maeklong* (pan-fried fish with lemongrass and cashew nuts), complex soups and starter boxes such as *Goong Frong* Beer (prawns with coconut beer batter). Close your eyes for a minute and the noise of scraping chairs and fire-scented aromas from the kitchen could easily have you believing you're in Bangkok. A word of warning though: there's no reservations policy, so bring an umbrella in case you have to wait outside in the rain.

55–57 Lothian Road, EH1 2DJ
Other location: Old Town
tingthai-caravan.com
@tingthaicaravanedinburgh
☺

Ting Thai Caravan

Cairngorm Coffee

Cairngorm Coffee

With countertop-to-ceiling windows, a crossroads location perfect for meet-ups and a curated coffee menu, this minimal but beloved neighbourhood café in the West End is invariable packed with good reason. Since the company started in the wild expanses of Cairngorms National Park (an unlikely destination for a roaster, admittedly), Edinburgh has become the coffee brand's spiritual home – nowadays there are two other locations in the capital. This Melville Place outpost is the original and it's the quintessential coffee drinker's establishment: bar stools meet large windows, a sleek server's counter tenders a cake, brownie or sandwich to go with your latte or espresso, and it's a retreat from the often wet and grey reality outside; here, the colour scheme is brilliant white and warm pine.

1 Melville Place, EH3 7PR
Other locations: New Town,
St James Quarter
cairngorm.coffee
@cairngormcoffeeco

Milk

There's no shortage of ten-a-penny cafés in Edinburgh nowadays, but this blissfully uncommercial company first lead the pack in 2010 – and with a laudably sustainable approach to using locally grown and organically farmed food too. Once you've wrapped up your umbrella, take a table by the window and take pity on those rushing to and from work or nearby Haymarket Station. For breakfast or brunch, it's time for veggie and vegan plates of halloumi, avocado, spinach and eggs, while later in the day the kitchen's mood-board changes: the soups, sandwiches and salads here help fuel the office workers of the nearby financial district.

232 Morrison Street, Haymarket,
EH3 8EA
Other locations: Stockbridge
(pop up in Inverleith Park), Newhaven
cafemilk.co.uk
@thecafemilk

The Voyage of Buck

A case is often made by West End locals that William Street is the most beautiful in the city. Its short stretch of Georgian-era townhouses comes replete with cobblestones, seasonal fairy lights and shops, and the chance of an encounter with one of the best drinking spots in the city is impressively high. One such place is this decadent, quasi-bohemian bar and restaurant, with an ever-changing cocktail menu that flip-flops between motif cities like Paris, Havana and Shanghai. Overall, the concept is tied to the backstory of fictitious William 'Buck' Clarence – a Phileas Fogg type, by way of Portobello – but that's secondary to the design (artichoke-scalloped wallpaper, bistro chairs and marble-top bar) and food (small and large plates, from tacos to buns to gnocchis). You'll love it for the travel 'artefacts' supposedly curated by Buck himself and when you've had your fill of cocktails from Istanbul or Venice, know that the owners run two equally-fun places across the city. There's Hamilton's in Stockbridge and The Blackbird in Tollcross.

29–31 William Street, EH3 7NF
thevoyageofbuckedinburgh.co.uk
@thevoyageofbuck
🏛️ ☺

Teuchters

Perhaps the oddest drinking challenge in Edinburgh can be found at this West End bar which makes a great deal out of its 120-plus single malt whisky collection. Not every patron wants to take on The Hoop of Destiny – for a nominal fee you can throw a ring at the whisky bottles and drink whichever one it lands on, no matter the price – but it sets the tone for this good-natured pub. Rugby is also a common theme and few pubs are livelier for watching the Scotland national team play at Murrayfield Stadium nearby. At such times, or when a game is on TV, it's standing room only, so come early to grab a table if you can, otherwise it's loitering on the cobbles outside. Away from single malts and scrums, there's a terrific selection of Scottish beers on tap and the food has a Highland feel; stand-outs are mugs of Haggis, Neeps and Tatties and Cullen Skink. And, in case you were wondering, a 'Teuchter' is a southern Scots nickname for someone from the north. Fittingly, the co-owners are from Angus and Caithness.

26 William Street, EH7 3NH
teuchtersbar.co.uk
@teuchtersbar

Cloisters Bar

Holy is the drinker who comes to this much-loved sanctuary of a real ale pub close to Edinburgh's student ground zero, The Meadows. It opened in 1995 in the historical former All Saints Parsonage and is a godly place for a pint, with wooden seats and tables crowded together as if set for a gathering congregation. From the dusty chalkboard showcasing the ever-changing score of house kegs and guest beers on tap to the 70-odd malt whiskies to nurse by the stove on a wet day, the pub is an illustration of how religion can be forsaken in the name of regeneration and the menu offers up a holy trinity of flavours – the main events are divine burgers, loaded fries and pub classics. As backdrops go, you can't help but feel a little blessed to have sought it out.

26 Brougham Steet, EH3 9JH
cloistersbar.com
@cloistersedinburgh

Cloisters

The Jolly Botanist

Edinburgh hit peak gin a few years ago at a time when the botanical spirit was booming, but this specialist Haymarket bar takes its gin just as seriously now. Those seeking a curated aperitif are looked after by trendy mixologists who know the difference between their juniper and coriander, angelica and orris, while if you're a gin virgin you can play Russian roulette with whatever your wallet is ready for. That could be a floral Viking gin from Orkney with orange peel, or a straight-from-the-source citrusy gin from Lind & Lime made in Leith. Next to the bar you'll find a kitchen serving Scottish small plates with flavours running the gamut from the humble Scotch Egg to Grilled Octopus to Short Rib. To continue your adventure in gin, make a date with a demonstration at the Edinburgh Gin Distillery, based around the corner on Rutland Street (see page 72).

256–260 Morrison Street, EH3 8DT
thejollybotanist.co.uk
@thejollybotanist

The Wee Vault Tasting Room

If brash chain pubs just aren't for you and you like a bit more attention when it comes to ordering your modern beers, then head to this tasting room and bottle shop near Haymarket train station – it's only got enough room for about a dozen drinkers. The clue is in the name, of course, but despite its dinky size – there's little more than a strip of counter seating, a bottle-stacked fridge and the custom-built 24 beer taps themselves – this place delivers big on flavour and style. Sour beers brewed at the bigger taproom in Portobello are the speciality, but it would be worth nothing without the right beer guide behind the bar. Pick from tart peach and mango beers, or sweet ones muddled with white chocolate and raspberry or choc chip cookie dough. Then think where you're heading next before you get too tipsy.

7A West Maitland Street, EH12 5DS
vaultcity.co.uk
@weevaultedi
🗔

Library of Mistakes

This quirky attraction is in the business of promoting better financial ideas for us to live by and is an oddity by anyone's measure. The dream is for the site to one day become the world's best business and finance library, but for now it's a free and peaceful place of reading rooms for studying the mistakes that have been made throughout financial and business history. Minutes from crowd-thronged Princes Street, the atmosphere couldn't be more different here as scholars, students and those keen to learn more about the financial madness of the world we live in sit in silence, pondering tomes of economic theory and corporate history. True, it's hardly your usual city-break highlight, but if you time your visit around one of the monthly lectures you could listen in to one of the world's sharpest economic minds.

33A Melville Street Lane, West End, EH3 7QB
libraryofmistakes.com
@EdinburghLoM
⊛

The Georgian House

Edinburgh locals are spoilt when it comes to beautiful buildings and townhouses – the streetscapes of both the Old and New Towns are UNESCO World Heritage wonders, after all. One place many overlook, though, is this fabulous period manor in the heart of the West End and it's a world apart from the square outside. The drawing and dining rooms have the paintings, costumes and epoch-defining furnishings of the 1800s; the kitchen and servants' quarters shed light on the 'below stairs' inequality that was once rampant across Britain. As well as the priceless collections of porcelain, glass and silver, this grand house of luxury regularly welcomes exhibitions that showcase the whims, fashions and tastes of the time. Fittingly, there's often a lack of affordable housing in Edinburgh, so it's funny to think that this prime slice of real estate was originally only worth £1,800 in 1796.

7 Charlotte Square, EH2 4DR
Closed Jan & Feb (see website)
nts.org.uk
@nts_georgianhouse
🏛☺

Scottish National Gallery of Modern Art

Scottish National Gallery of Modern Art

A walk to this unmissable art museum with two distinct personalities – Modern One and Modern Two lie directly across the road from each other – stirs an appetite for art, and you'll be rewarded with works from such top-notch masters as Picasso, Tracey Emin and Andy Warhol. In the permanent collection, native son of Leith Eduardo Paolozzi's sculpture studio has been recreated, while the tutored eye will recognize works by the likes of Henri Matisse, Joan Miró, Salvador Dalí and Roy Lichtenstein amid a collection that hangs heavy with Scottish talent. The rain means you'll have time to explore the temporary exhibitions at leisure, but you'll likely have to come back under brighter skies to explore the grounds, both of which are ambushed by dozens of sculptures and installations. What you won't be able to miss, though, is Charles Jencks' swirling landform that's been terraformed into existence on the front lawn.

75 Belford Road, EH4 3DR
nationalgalleries.org
@natgaliessco
☺ ✪

Edinburgh Printmakers

For a glimpse of gentrification at its finest, come to Fountainbridge: it's almost unrecognizable to how the area was a few years ago and design lovers have taken to the Edinburgh Printmakers with whole-hearted enthusiasm since the art studio moved into the neighbourhood from its former headquarters in the New Town back in 2019. This new lease of life in a beautiful heritage building vacated by a rubber company and brewery has seen the studio go from strength to strength and walk-ins are welcome to explore the eye-popping exhibitions, vegan café and shop. Courses run from lithography to screen-printing, while the multi-level balconied space is a mixture of open-access studios for invited artists and publishing partners and viewing galleries for you to witness world-class printing in action.

Castle Mills, 1 Dundee Street, EH3 9FP
edinburghprintmakers.co.uk
@edinburghprintmakers
☺ ✪

Edinburgh Gin Distillery

When the ducks are outside splashing in the downpour and Princes Street is a sea of umbrellas, this gin company tucked down a staircase on the corner of Lothian Road is an absolute revelation. It's true that Edinburgh – and Scotland, for that matter – is hardly short of fine makers nowadays, but Edinburgh Gin began in 2010 and was well ahead of the curve. Inside, you'll find something more unusual than most distillery tours, as there are various options with which to fill your day: learn the botanicals-to-bottle process while tasting five gins and gin liqueurs; take part in a more immersive cocktail experience; or, for those who like to think outside the box, there's gin and chocolate pairing sessions. After a few drinks, perhaps of seaside gin with a salty kiss or rhubarb or gin liqueur, it's cosiness incarnate.

1A Rutland Street, EH1 2AD
edinburghgin.com
@edinburghgin

8 Yards

If kilts could talk they'd tell you about all the famous celebrities with sartorial style who have donned the traditional tartan wear over the decades. From homegrown Scots like Sir Sean Connery, Gerard Butler, Sam Heughan and Ewan McGregor to Vin Diesel, Samuel L. Jackson and Muhammad Ali (who donned one back in 1963), the kilt can look at home on anyone's legs. This bijou kilt boutique in Haymarket runs in an old-school way, with made-to-measure men's and ladieswear fittings, but with modern 21st-century tartans and matching clan gifts. Such is its success, in fact, that the boutique has moved into Scottish homewares, as well as pocket watches, brooches, jewellery, hats and handbags. In summer – the height of the Scottish wedding season – the shop bursts at the seams (literally and figuratively), with last-minute ex-hire orders and fittings, so if you're in the market for a kilt to take home, avoid the Thursday-to-Saturday stampede.

54–56 Haymarket Terrace, EH12 5LA
8yards.co.uk
@eightyards

Frontiers Woman

The family behind this independent womenswear boutique just off super-hip William Street could be described as the best dressed in the West End. First opened more than 30 years ago, the shop is a stalwart of all-ages of Edinburgh fashion and it's known for its hard-to-find garments and brand exclusives to Edinburgh and Scotland. There are footwear and accessories too, and you'll be hard pushed to find someone who knows more about how to dress the right way on a wet day than the owner and former knitwear designer Jane Forbes. Handily, for male shoppers feeling left out in the cold, sibling fashion boutique Frontiers Man is just across the road – and it's run by Forbes' partner.

16B Stafford Street, EH3 7AU
frontiers-woman.com
@frontierswoman.edinburgh

UNIONgallery

Between Princes Street and the Water of Leith, the famous sights
are few but there is this contemporary art gallery where you
can pop in, view pieces you won't find elsewhere, and – if you're
wallet is weighing you down – leave with an artwork from an
up-and-coming new artist or already established big name. The
gallery is spread over two floors and among the mixed media
artworks created in tribute to the city's Old and New Town
architecture you might see something else entirely different:
how about a Raku-fired penguin, a tartan hare made from steel
or an almost life-scale cold-cast bronze fur seal? While browsing,
keep an eye out for pieces signed by local contemporary artist
Alison Auldjo – she's the owner.

4 Drumsheugh Place, West End, EH3 7PT
uniongallery.co.uk
@uniongallery1
⊛

Paper Tiger

Positivity kits, dinosaur puppets, shark-beaded bracelets, gin and tonic soap... these are all genuine novelties for sale in this quirky gift shop in the heart of the West End. Come to see the full range of cards, mugs, personalized moleskins and retro knick-knacks for yourself – note, Tintin and Snoopy feature heavily – and you'll find it hard to resist leaving without something. It's a labour of love for owner Michael Apter, who personally works with artists for the gift cards and hand-selects the cuddly toys to sell, and the store and its sibling on nearby Lothian Road are run sustainably and with an environmentally conscious ethos. A case in point: trees are planted to offset the store's carbon footprint.

6A Stafford Street, EH3 7AU
Other location: Tollcross
papertiger.co.uk
@shoppapertiger
☺

Rogue Flowers

Like tumbling down the rabbit hole or stepping through the wardrobe, this West End flower shop was conceived as a kind of indoor neighbourhood garden and flower cabinet to showcase its owners' love of floral artistry. Indeed, it's hard to walk down William Street and not spot it, as its one-of-a-kind flower bouquets fall out of the front door, almost taking over the pavement. Inside, it's just as wild and chaotic and there are flowers, posies and greens for any occasion, and even if you don't actually need a flamboyant preserved flower wreath or orchid planter the shop sells a fine line in soy wax candles with scents that, apparently, bring the blossom-scented streets of the Old and New Towns and The Meadows to life.

5A William Street, West End, EH3 7NG
rogueflowers.co.uk
@rogueflowers

South

The rush to Edinburgh's crowded guidebook sights often bypasses some of the city's most alluring neighbourhoods and many of the most fashionable are in the south. Best-in-class cafés, bakeries and restaurants congregate on the streets fanning out from The Meadows and Bruntsfield Links, with Bruntsfield and Morningside taking the lion's share of places that you'll want to top your rainy day list. This part of town is also home to the southern suburbs of Marchmont and Newington, both of which envelope the sprawling University of Edinburgh and give rise to studenty pubs, bars and cultural spaces that provide plenty of diversions.

Elliott's

Elliott's

Take one cookbook writer and food stylist (Jess Elliott Dennison), add one artist (Phillippa Henley), and you have the recipe for this Marchmont café, bakery and studio that has one eye on morning cakes and scones and the other on kitchenware, store cupboard ingredients and cookery demonstrations. The café and studio are a few doors apart, so it's the former where you really get a sense of the local community and what life is like in one of Edinburgh's loveliest residential areas. The cakes and bakes are of the come-back-for-more variety, ranging from Grapefruit Amaretti and Prune, Maple and Spelt Scones to Fennel Sausage Rolls and Vegetable Galettes. For the more angelic, there are teas, coffees and organic juices, plus preserves and pickles to pop in your bag for home and signed copies of Jess's books for that extra special someone. Should it stop raining, the nearby Meadows comes alive with joggers and dog walkers – the perfect place to work off any potential calories.

27 Sciennes Road, Marchmont, EH9 1NX
elliottsedinburgh.com
@elliotts_edinburgh
⊟ ☺

Union Brew Lab

Coffee shops are no longer coffee shops these days and this glorious artisan roastery-cum-lifestyle coffee shop is a case in point. It's both a coffee provisions store and a training lab, with barista courses, filter brewing masterclasses and speciality experiences to help you up your coffee game. There's plenty still to enjoy for those who want a simple latte or cappuccino though, and the stripped-back stop is a magnet for students from the nearby University of Edinburgh campus and for those who love pastries, sweets and cakes. Get excited about the cinnamon buns or vegan doughnuts and pair them with a filter batch brew from roast Ethiopian beans or a nitro cold brew, then consider running across to the nearby National Museum of Scotland, where you could happily spend a few hours until it dries off.

6–8 South College Street, EH8 9AA
brewlabcoffee.co.uk
@brewlabcoffee

Bross Bagels

Montreal in Canada may be widely acknowledged as the original home of the wood-fired, honey-water boiled and baked bagel, but you'll also find some of Europe's most authentic sesame- and poppy-seed holey grails being sliced and toasted in this wallet-friendly Bruntsfield deli. The bagels are served with as much substance as they are style and you can pick from healthy options (Chicken Salad, Smashed Avocado) or deep New York-style fillings such as Pastrami and Monterey Jack, Cream Cheese and Salmon, or Schnitzel and Marinara Sauce. Owner and actor Larah Bross (aka Mama Bross) is from Montreal originally and, as well as this branch in Bruntsfield, there are now a number of Bross Bagels across the city: praise be indeed that somehow bagels taste better when it's cold and wet outside.

165A Bruntsfield Place, EH10 4DG
Other locations: Portobello, Stockbridge, St James Quarter
brossbagels.com
@bross_bagels
☺

Söderberg

Swedes obsess over 'fika' (an almost medicinal custom involving little more than a daily dose of coffee and cake) and a little window onto this transported ritual is the main draw at this institution in the Quartermile. All comers, from families with pushchairs to students, joggers and dog walkers escaping the rain, turn it into a sort of communal living room while bonding over coffee served with fresh bakes, waffles and cardamom buns (Swedish staple *Kardemummabullar*). Later in the day, the bakery shifts up a gear to do Sourdough Pizzas, *Smörrebröd* platters and open-faced sandwiches – all which can be coupled with a Lingonberry Cosmopolitan or Fika Martini (made with coffee liquor and Swedish vodka). This is a typical Edinburgh café – unpretentious and welcoming.

27 Simpson Loan, EH3 9GG
Other locations: Stockbridge,
Morningside, Leith
soderberg.co.uk
@soderbergbakery
🏢 ☺

Harajuku Kitchen

For the most part, Japanese restaurants in Edinburgh are low-key affairs, but this southside favourite in Bruntsfield turns the volume up on sushi, sashimi, and udon. There are plenty of echoes of the Land of the Rising Sun in the decor – cartoon wall murals, tatami screens, balloon-shaped lampshades, a painting of spring blossoms – and the menu leans heavily on chef-owner Kaori Simpson's upbringing in the Fukuoka region of Japan (though her Mum worked as a chef in Osaka). Indecisive diners will love the choice – *Takoyaki* (octopus dough balls with Katsu-Mayo), Okinawa-style Pork Belly, *Tonkatsu* (panko-crumbed pork cutlet) – but if your tongue is calling out for a jolt, order a Meat or Aubergine *Karei* (curry). With authentic *Donburi* (rice bowls with miso), *Mentsuyu* (noodle soup with kelp dashi stock) and *Chirashi Don* (speciality sushi rice bowls) on the menu, you might well feel inclined to try it all. Hold that thought: there are Apple Gyozas, Sticky Rice Cakes and *Dorayaki* with Green Tea Custard for afters. Elsewhere, for a grab-and-go when hiding out from the rain in the St James Quarter, the restaurant has a dinky street food container on Little King Street.

10 Gillespie Place, EH10 4HS
harajukukitchen.co.uk
@harajukukitchen
🏢 ☺

The Sheep Heid Inn

Anyone for a game of skittles? If the weather isn't up to much, then this historical pub in Duddingston with its own indoor alley with original ball return track is unbeatable for good old-fashioned fun with a crowd. Legend has it that it's one of Edinburgh's oldest surviving watering holes, not that it shows on the food or drinks menu. Expect pub staples like Beef Brisket Pie, Line-caught Cod and Chips and steaks from the rotisserie grill. You'll want to book ahead for the popular Sunday lunch – six are on offer every weekend, from Pork Belly to Fig and Dolcelatte, and the out-of-town location is as charming as it is discreet. In fact, when she was resident at the Palace of Holyrood at the foot of the Royal Mile, it was one of Her Majesty Queen Elizabeth's favourite pub stops – once, she took a window seat with a small entourage and ordered a fillet of seabass, stunning regulars in the process.

43–45 The Causeway, EH15 3QA
thesheepheidedinburgh.co.uk
@thesheepheid
🏛☺

Tipsy Midgie

If you've spent any time in the Scottish countryside, then you'll already be familiar with the nation's blood-sucking flying insect – the terrorist of summer, the Highland midge. This bar takes its name from the little horrors and it can be found on a quiet and thankfully midge-free street in the shadow of Arthur's Seat, Edinburgh's dormant volcanic barb. It's set up as a whisky and gin drinkery, with extensive menus dedicated to the five whisky regions of Scotland, as well as the worlds of gin, Champagne and prosecco. You can just pop in for a drink to meet owner Colin Hinds – he claims to put the 'dram' in 'dramatic' – but if you want a boozy experience that you can only get in Edinburgh, then keep an eye out for the bar's regular events, some of which include whisky and chocolate pairings and distillery discovery nights. For the ultimate one-for-the-road on a dismal night, order a 'Can and a Dram' – a blended whisky paired with a craft beer from a local microbrewer.

67 St Leonard's Hill, EH8 9SB
tipsymidgie.com
@tipsymidgie
🏛

Paradise Palms

For a gasp of tropical air and ambience amid the rain, head into this gloriously colourful tartan Tiki bar next to studenty Teviot Square, with fruit cocktails and vegan food on tap. This is the place to let your hair down with a Piña Colada, Mai Tai or Jamaican Rum Punch no matter the time – or go full Scottish with a Buckfast Daiquiri (Cuban rum topped with a balanced fusion of lime, sugar and medicinal tonic wine – a drink so popular there's an area outside Glasgow dubbed the 'Buckfast Triangle'). Around you, the decor is equally spirit-lifting: consider hot pink neon signs, ribbons of rainbow bunting, pot plants and enough tropical fruit to make you think you're in the Caribbean, not Caledonia. Food-wise, you're here for dirty veggie and vegan soul food served in diner baskets – pick from Plant-based Burgers, Loaded Fries and the house signature Buffalo Cauliflower. Staying out late? Then there are regular gigs and late night DJ sets.

41 Lothian Street, EH1 1HB
theparadisepalms.com
@edinburghpalms

Bennets Bar

Stuck beneath bruised-purple skies in Tollcross? Head to this historical Victorian-era pub that's been serving since the turn of the 20th century in 1906. You're coming for the beer and banter, but also the beautiful interiors (unchanged for almost a century) and belt-loosening pizzas – or, perhaps, you might be warming-up pre- or post-theatre when attending a show at the chocolate box King's Theatre next door. As you enter, you'll be awed by the beautiful oak gantry, built to house the boozer's collection of fine whiskies and spirits, but also for the museum-piece arched mirrors, stained glass windows, and original snug – so-designed to hide those like women, priests and policemen who didn't want to be seen drinking in public. Not that anyone has this problem today, of course: expect Bennets to pack out in the evening and on weekends when it's often elbow-room only.

8 Leven Street, EH3 9LG
bennetsbar.co.uk
@bennetsbar

Canny Man's

One of the oldest pubs in Edinburgh and with enough antiques, trinkets and curios on display to fill a museum, this fifth-generation Morningside institution with alcoves and private rooms is a picture to be seen. There are two dyed-in-the-wool pubs. One has a woodwork gantry that dates back to original owner James Kerr in the early 1870s; the other, a locals and lounge-like feel. The scrumptious restaurant celebrates fresh, local produce and is particularly known for its seafood, *smørrebrød* sandwiches and Sunday lunches. If you've ever heard of celebrated Cornish TV chef Rick Stein, then he described it as 'the best pub in the world', plus its Bloody Mary (made with a secret ingredient) is the best in the city. Truly, a weekend place to wallow in when it rains.

237 Morningside Road, EH10 4QU
cannymans.co.uk
@thecannymans

Holyrood Distillery

Holyrood Distillery

Few things make an Edinburgh pub better than a good selection of single malt whisky, so the arrival of the first city-centre distillery in the capital for more than 100 years in 2019 was greeted with open arms. You'll have to wait for its first whisky distillation (all Scotch must be matured in oak casks for a three-year minimum, with most distillers opting for a seven- to 10-year spirit evolution), but that's not stopped this award-winning operation from running terrific tastings and tours of its production floor of mash tuns, fermentation tanks, wash backs and stills – and all within easy reach of the Royal Mile (see the website for tour details). To help with the spirit samples, the distillery also makes gin and rum.

19 St Leonard's Lane, EH8 9SH
holyrooddistillery.co.uk
@holyrooddistillery

Summerhall

Across Edinburgh, there are plenty of projects that prove you can combine style, culture and do-gooding, and Summerhall is at the vanguard of the arts scene. The former home of the Royal School of Veterinary Studies, the mini campus is now home to live music, theatre, performance, film and visual arts, as well as a number of sustainably-minded start-ups. Among them are Barney's Beer microbrewery and Pickering's Gin, both of which you can sample in The Gallery Bar and The Royal Dick Bar, named after the founder of the vet school William Dick (for those of a certain age, the former school will always affectionately be called 'The Dick' in homage). As well as a jam-packed programme of cutting-edge events throughout the year, Summerhall is home to the regular Edinburgh Ceilidh Club and plays a major role in hosting dozens of shows during August's world-famous Fringe Festival.

1 Summerhall, Newington, EH9 1PL
summerhall.co.uk
@summerhallery

Surgeon's Hall Museums

From Greyfriar's Kirkyard, where J.K. Rowling first spotted tombstones etched with the name Mr. Potter and others that she absorbed into her wizarding saga, to the subterranean streets of once plague-ridden Mary's King's Close, Edinburgh is undoubtedly a city of curious attractions. Chief among these is this collection of museums made up of the Wohl Pathology Museum, History of Surgery Museum and Dental Collection. Inside, you'll be treated (or tortured, depending on your outlook) to abnormal skulls, body parts, skeletons, surgical instruments and spine-winding anatomical tools. Stories and myths tied to many of the objects are legion, with the one associated with the city's notorious bodysnatchers Burke and Hare the most famous. The criminal pair murdered 16 people to sell as body parts to Edinburgh's anatomy schools in 1827 and one particularly grisly exhibit is Burke's death mask – it's scarred with marks from the hangman's noose.

Nicolson Street, EH8 9DW
museum.rcsed.ac.uk
@surgeonshall
☺

Dominion Cinema

Dominion Cinema

It's difficult not to be blind-sided by this truly Art Deco cinema when trying to escape the rain in Morningside. With its name written in scarlet-red neon lettering down one side of the building, this family-run independent cinema makes quite an impression before you've even pushed your way through its swing doors. You'll be following in fine footsteps too, as the cinema was once a key showcase for the now-defunct Edinburgh International Film Festival – the likes of Cary Grant, Jude Law, Sigourney Weaver, Dame Judy Dench and Sir Billy Connolly have all trotted along the red carpet here. They make an appearance in the foyer's hall of fame, but you're really here for the first class Gold Screen, with its plush armchairs, free Pringles and bowls of sweeties, and full-table evening service. Check out its website for the latest screenings, many of which are classics, indies and arthouse flicks.

Newbattle Terrace, EH10 4RT
dominioncinema.co.uk
@dominioncinema
🏛 ☺

The Cameo

When the weather shifts in Edinburgh, it moves fast, so this century-old arthouse cinema in Tollcross is the perfect escape for a few hours. If you're a bona fide film fan, what you won't get is mainstream Hollywood blockbusters – more overlooked rarities, indies, cult re-releases, double bills and European and Asian flicks that champion story over special effects. The space has developed over the decades and as well as three screens there's now an Art Deco-influenced bar for chewing over the latest releases. The building itself first opened as a cinema pre-First World War in 1914 and originally had a mirrored screen – the first of its kind in the country. For proper cineastes, The Cameo plays a starring role in *The Illusionist*, a feature-length French animation directed by Sylvain Chomet.

38 Home Street, EH3 9LZ
picturehouses.com
@thecameocinema
🏛 ☺

Halibut and Herring

Whisk yourself to this gift store in Bruntsfield and feel your day brighten up the instant you step inside. The retina-filling look is of pastel pinks, powder blues and tropical greens – almost as if the store has parachuted in from sunnier climes – and it's as warm and welcoming a shop as you'd hope to find under gloomy skies. Shelves are stacked with bowls detailed with Sicilian lemons and primary colour fish, while art prints are of watermelon cocktails and the range of ceramics runs through a Pantone spectrum from scarlet red to marigold to navy blue. There is a sense that there's a gift for every occasion here and a lot that you could spend your money on.

108 Bruntsfield Place, EH10 4ES
halibutandherring.co.uk
@halibutandherring

Totty Rocks

Tired of fast fashion and so-called disposable fashion from the high-street retailers? Then this Bruntsfield neighbourhood boutique-meets–design studio is just for you. It's the brainchild of Holly Mitchell and Lynsey Byrne and it's a laidback showroom of both the pair's made-to-measure tailoring and off-the-peg handiworks, from wrap dresses and balloon sleeve tops to more practical clothing for the unpredictable Edinburgh weather – stalker capes and tartan trenches with military-style collars to keep the cold and rain out are a speciality. A chat feels like a personalized shopping experience, and if you're in the mood for a whole new makeover then don't hold back: sewing herringbone tweed or leather is what this independent fashion label thrives on.

45–47 Barclay Place, EH10 4HW
tottyrocks.co.uk
@tottyrocksltd

Curiouser

The story behind this delightful gift shop is the kind of revelation that gives unfulfilled careerists dangerous delusions about jacking in the day job. Owners Laura Clifford and Ian Staples felt similarly restless when they had a lightbulb moment and opened their first independent boutique on Broughton Street in Leith in 2012 and now a decade later the pair run two successful stores – including this one in Bruntsfield. Full to the brim with spectacle, there are gift cards, jewellery, homewares and art prints and whether you're a plant or book lover or stationery or sock connoisseur this emporium has something for you.

106 Bruntsfield Place, EH10 4LA
Other location: Broughton
curiouserandcuriouser.com
@curiousershop

Lighthouse Bookshop

Edinburgh was the world's first UNESCO City of Literature, but not every bookshop fits the brief of a Waterstones or W H Smith. As radical as they come, Lighthouse in Newington is a leading purveyor of left-wing and Scottish politics, with a hefty selection of titles devoted to intersectional feminism, revolutionary history, environmentalism, LGBT+ writing, poetry and translated fiction – voices from the margins are championed in a way that no other space in the city can manage. The walls are lined with an eclectic selection of some 10,000 books and as an unapologetically outspoken voice the female team in charge run provocative weekly events, as well as the Book Fringe in August and the Radical Book Fair in November.

43–45 West Nicolson Street, EH8 9DB
lighthousebookshop.com
@lighthousebks

The Edinburgh Bookshop

South of the green parklands of The Meadows, Bruntsfield is defined by well-kept townhouses, restaurant and pub opportunities and fantastic independent retailers like this homely bookshop. For locals, it's a place equally known for tea, biscuits and dog cuddles as it is its shelves jam-packed with prize-winning fiction. You'll also find notebooks, knick-knacks and staff always willing to recommend the book that's keeping them up late at night. Come for a browse, or eavesdrop on one of the regular book clubs or story-time sessions – otherwise, check in advance for author signings and talks.

219 Bruntsfield Place, EH10 4DH
edinburghbookshop.com
@theedinburghbookshop
☺

East

Every capital city has a genre-bending upstart neighbourhood somewhere on its map and Edinburgh is no different. Leith, which was once a port town in its own right to the northeast, dominates much of the conversation in the city with its newfangled craft brewers, farm-to-fork restaurants, Fair Trade coffee roasters and independent bookshops, and this is where to head for what's new and next in the city. Next to Leith on the map, southeast along the North Sea shoreline, is Portobello, an area that's popular with beachcombers, sun bathers and swimmers. But this cold Hawaii isn't the only thing Porty has going for it – come for bagels, brews, beers and books.

The Little Chartroom

Nowhere in the New Town gives you a better sense of the importance of Leith to the evolution of Edinburgh than this perfectly-formed restaurant and wine bar. It first opened on Leith Walk and has since moved to Bonnington Road, but the cooking is still among the country's finest and the ever-changing tasting menus are a wellspring of local produce. Behind it all is Roberta Hall-McCarron, the city's most celebrated female chef, and her front-of-house partner Shaun, and while the accents are firmly east-coast Scottish, the ambition is world-beating. Hungry? Then how about Hogget Chop, Plaice Bourguignon, Sage and Chestnut Gnocchi or Mackerel Escabeche? A restaurant this terrific demands reservations and – should you not luck out with a last-minute meal because of the weather – you could also try the couple's other showstopper. Eleanore moved into the dinky space left behind by The Little Chartroom (30–31 Albert Place, EH7 5HN) and has equally worthy small plates and seasonal menus.

14 Bonnington Road, EH6 5JD
thelittlechartroom.com
@thelittlechartroom
🗓

Alby's

Alby's

Sandwiches are officially back in fashion and nowhere more so than at this heroic café offering OTT signature 'big hot' sandwiches that by rights should be on every visitor's bucket-list when visiting the city. It's popular for a reason with Portobello locals and Alby's sandwich gurus serve up colourful doorstops of bread filled to overflowing with flavours that would be worth framing and putting on show in a gallery. Top choices include: Ham Hock, Pea and Pickled Onion Fritter with Malt Vinegar Mayo; Crab Cakes, Whipped Cod's Roe and Dill Crème Fraîche; and Charred Tenderstem Broccoli with Anchovies, Salsa Verde and Burrata Cream. Far from your typical sandwich place, the best bit is the tutti-frutti selection of meat and non-meat fillings that change as often as the weather. Note, it has limited opening hours so check the website or socials.

8 Portland Place, Portobello, EH6 6LA
albysleith.co.uk
@albys_leith
📖 ☺

The Kitchin

Skip breakfast (or lunch) and take a deep breath before visiting this game-changing Leith restaurant on The Shore. Almost single-handedly responsible for shaking up destination dining in the city during the mid-2000s, it's the brainchild of appropriately-named Michelin-star chef Tom Kitchin, who's now gone on to open a handful of other terrific restaurants and gastropubs in the capital (including The Scran & Scallie in Stockbridge, see page 34). When the celebs are in the capital they come here, so you'll need to book in advance for its surprise tasting menus, and your fellow guests are a well-heeled bunch, so you'll want to dress the part too. It isn't snooty though – just comfy – and food-wise you're here for nature-to-plate seasonal dishes like Pig's Head and Langoustine, Highland Wagyu Beef Tartare, and Veal Sweetbreads. The Kitchin team loves wild game, so at the right time, the menu swells with plates of hare, hand-dived scallops and loin of roe deer. World-class cuisine? Yes, but you'll pay for it.

78 Commercial Quay, Leith, EH6 6LX
thekitchin.com
@thekitchin
📖

Heron

Leith, where a growing number of relaxed restaurants really understand how to do culinary Scottishness justice, is not part of Edinburgh – at least locals successfully argue it counts otherwise. Among the chefs destined for greatness here are Tomás Gormley and Sam Yorke of Heron, who present their river-facing corner restaurant with an algae-green ceiling and lampshades that could double as bird nests (if anything, it's early proof they're good at subtlety). You'll also find a menu that is both bold and playful and hinged around a carousel of ever-changing dishes that – one day – might have Michelin star written all over them. Like raw scallop sloshed in Ajoblanco, or beef fillet cut like a slab of rock from Edinburgh Castle. A love of fresh Scottish produce is at the heart of what the chefs do and the food is truly wonderful, so you can be forgiven for dipping your beak right onto the plate just like the restaurant's namesake – perhaps to mop up the rest of a Plum Alaska dessert or Chocolate Morsel with Miso and Hazelnut.

91A Henderson Street, Leith, EH6 6ED
heron.scot
@heron.scot
🏛

Williams & Johnson

When the weather's bright, this is a linger-in-the-sun sort of place, with outdoor tables anchored on the Water of Leith riverside beside the historical Custom House. Visit in the rain though, and you'll want to duck through the courtyard into this grassroots café and micro-roaster, which shares headspace with Custom Lane, a co-working centre for design – hence it's manicured creative edge. The Williams and Johnson in question are Zach and Todd, two barista alumni from Leith's other great trailblazing coffee makers Artisan Roast (see page 38), and you're here for bold single origin coffees with character and seasonal espressos. The cakes, from cinnamon swirls to salted caramel cookies, and sourdough toasties ain't half bad either and if you love what you're tasting, there are brew kits and coffee subscriptions so the boys can send their small batch roasted beans straight to your home.

1 Customs Wharf, Leith, EH6 6AL
williamsandjohnson.com
@williams_and_johnson_coffee

Nauticus

It's almost unheard of to find a pub that can claim that nearly all of its drinks come from the city and country it's based in, but that's the case at this devoutly Scottish boozer in Leith. Owner Kyle Jamieson's claim is around 90 per cent of the drinks on the menu are from Scotland and – when this wasn't feasible – Scottish heritage or historical links to Leith were hunted down. What that means for you on a wet day is Edinburgh lagers and cask ales, Lothian botanical gins and Highland single malt whiskies, while there's no let up on the wine or sherry front either; Leith once specialized in bottle manufacturing, producing up to one million wine bottles a week. Away from Scotland's alcohol pedigree, the pub itself is stunning, with a wood-pannelled sheen and subtle hat tips to the area's nautical heritage: cue a life buoy, brass diving helmet and model frigate above the fireplace. With all this eye-candy and plenty of grog besides, it's a pub simply made for a modern-day pirate.

142 Duke Street, Leith, EH6 8HR
nauticusbar.co.uk
@nauticusbar

Lost in Leith

Ignore the name: this bricks-and-mortar outlet for Leith's beloved Campervan Brewery is no harder to find than any other drinking establishment in Edinburgh. It's a quick dash from the Water of Leith on a rainy day and the perfect spot for doing little more than supping an experimental pint with a paper or iPad. What sets it apart is this pub is also a fermentaria, a microbrew project centred around the on-site beer barrel-ageing and mixed fermentation process. It's not as nerdy as it sounds though, and the three centrepiece oak barrels from Cognac, France, add to the vibe, as does the chalkboard of specials and weird and wonderful IPAs and hoppy ales from around the globe. Try a Campervan favourite like a Leith Juice (orange-imbued session IPA) or Leith Pils (gluten-free keller pilsner) and bear in mind that no food is served (although you can call in a delivery from Pizza Geeks across the road – ask the bartender for recommendations).

82 Commercial Street, Leith, EH6 6LX
campervanbrewery.com
@lostinleithbar

The Lioness of Leith

The old-school arcade games, pinball, pop art murals and funky decor (how about a faux rhino head for starters?) have most visitors from the get-go. In trend-shaping Leith terms, this bar is also an old timer – opening a decade ago in 2013 – yet it keeps things here-and-now with twisted classic cocktails, support for local craft brewers and some of the most memorable burgers in the city. They're provided courtesy of Burger Mama (which now runs a takeaway shop opposite Haymarket Station) and you can pick from options like a terrific Flank and Skirt-steak Chilli Burger, a Buttermilk Kimchi classic or newfangled Panko-crumbed Mushroom Burger that blows others in the city out of the water. It's particularly lively at the weekend, but it's also kid- and dog-friendly, so families love it as much as good-time boys and girls.

21–25 Duke Street, Leith, EH6 8HH
thelionessofleith.co.uk
@thelionessofleith
🏢 ☺

Smith & Gertrude

Smith & Gertrude

Democracy in wine and cheese can be found at this emporium that celebrates viticulture and its favourite partner in all its many forms. Set back on the high street from shingle-sand Portobello Beach – hardly a location for a rainy day – it's a welcoming place for a glass and a nibble or a more immersive wine flight paired with soft, hard and blue cheeses that could keep you here for hours. The point of it all is to celebrate lesser-known wine regions and *vin du pays* of the highest order that don't quite fit the mould (a special mention here for orange wines), so you leave full to the brim, metaphorically speaking, but also better educated. The whole experience is better with a bottle, charcuterie plate and table of friends, of course, but the 'by the glass' menu is just as good and, if you think of yourself as an oenologist, then ask the staff for something old, odd or rare from the bar's little black book of wines.

254 Portobello High Street, Portobello, EH15 2AT
Other location: Stockbridge
smithandgertrude.com
@smithandgertrude

Spry

With the much talked-about extension of the Edinburgh Trams line soon to connect Leith Walk with Princes Street and the West End, joyous haunts like this wine bar on the ground floor of a typical Edinburgh Georgian house will be properly put on the map. Before then, relish the peace of one of the capital's most gratifying places for a glass of the grape – there's a selection of organic reds, whites and bubbles, but really you're here for the viticulture knowledge of owners Matt and Marzena. To line your stomach, there are fancier flavours than you'd expect in most wine bars and the ingredients are often from far beyond the Old World wine regions – expect dishes like Labneh with Pickled Cucumber, Carrot Kluski Dumplings and Pollock Paratha with Saffron. Otherwise, go the whole hog and order the five-course set menu with paired wines.

1 Haddington Place, New Town, EH7 4AE
sprywines.co.uk
@spry_wines

The Royal Yacht Britannia

Built in a shipyard in Glasgow, but now permanently anchored on the east coast, the former floating palace of HM Queen Elizabeth II and the Royals is a sight to behold amid the ramshackle Leith Docks. The interiors are indecently lovely, if a little dated and reflecting its four decades of service up to 1997 – but what a place to potter. Britannia conveyed the Royal Family on nearly 1,000 visits during its working life, hosting dignitaries from Winston Churchill to Ronald Reagan to Nelson Mandela, and it has the air of political and personal events that shaped both Queen Elizabeth II's reign – and the world around us. The main sights are in the belly of the ship, so no need to worry about the weather, and a tour of the five decks, swanky state apartments, crew's quarters and once steam-powered engine room offer up fascinating new perspectives on Britain's most famous family, regardless of whether you're a monarchist or not. To lord it up like a royal, sit where the Queen scoffed cream tea and Princes William and Harry played deck games in the Royal Deck Tea Room. It's the connoisseur's alternative to grabbing a bite from the surrounding Ocean Terminal shopping mall.

Ocean Drive, Leith, EH6 6JJ
royalyachtbritannia.co.uk
@royalyachtbritannia
☺

Edinburgh Sculpture Workshop

From the bronze Greyfriar's Bobby on George IV Bridge to statues of Sherlock Holmes and economist Adam Smith, Edinburgh is a storied city of sculpture. So it's fitting that Newhaven, close to where famous Pop Art sculptor and son of Leith Eduardo Paolozzi grew up, is the home of the Edinburgh Sculpture Workshop, an all-welcome hub of studios and creative goings on. Once here, check out the current exhibition or take a peek in the workshops, then grab a seat at Milk, a sibling to the rave-worthy café of the same name near Haymarket (see page 63). On occasion, there are workshops, work-in-progress exhibitions and descriptive talks, as well as fun days for families to make and play together.

21 Hawthornvale, Newhaven, EH6 4JT
edinburghsculpture.org
@eswsculpture
☺ ✪

alien rock

Ready to work up a sweat? This one-of-a-kind rock-climbing gym is for those who love a natural high. Opened as Scotland's first dedicated indoor climbing centre, it can be found inside a vaulted church overlooking the chess-piece lighthouse of Newhaven Harbour and is as much for beginners and kids, as it is for experts who know the difference between a bolt and a belay. There are some 400 possible combinations of routes, from easy bouldering sections to far gnarlier top-roping sections with wild overhangs. If you become hooked, or you're after less fear factor, then it's also worth seeking out Alien Bloc, the sibling centre for bouldering on Dunedin Street – here the walls don't exceed 4.7m (15.4 ft) in height and ropes aren't required.

8 Pier Place, Newhaven, EH6 4LP
alienrock.co.uk
@alienrock_bloc
☺

Leith Theatre

During the Second World War, German bombers intending to take out vital supply lines on Leith Docks mistakenly hit the main auditorium of this historic theatre – and yet nearly 80 years later it's still going strong. The theatre has had a chequered history to say the least; despite hosting such artists as AC/DC, Thin Lizzy and Kraftwerk in the 1970s and hosting the Edinburgh International Festival through the 1980s, it was mothballed in 1988. Thankfully, the threat of site redevelopment galvanized the local community and the landmark theatre has now reopened for regular concerts and TV broadcasts, and to host festivals. Check listings in advance before visiting Leith and you never know – you might end up moshing down the front of an unforgettable gig.

28–30 Ferry Road, Leith, EH6 4AE
leiththeatre.co.uk
@leiththeatre
🏛

The Biscuit Factory

Take the relic of a post-war biscuit factory and the neighbouring warehouse once occupied by a soap and chemical company from the 1900s and the result is one of the most exciting community spaces and venues in Scotland. Now home to dozens of creative industries, its inner sanctum has industrial fixtures and fittings, steel pillars, skylights and vintage window frames, while the spaces are filled on an ad-hoc basis with markets, pop-up bars and diners, electro DJ nights, record launches and photo shoots. It's a contender for the hippest place in the city, but while there's a buzzy community spread across its lower and upper floor offices – think a baker, hot sauce maker, distiller and coffee roaster – you'll need to check the events listings before turning up.

4–6 Anderson Place, Bonnington, EH6 5NP
biscuitfactory.co.uk
@biscuitfactoryedin
🏛

Topping & Company

Located at the top of Leith Walk, this perennially popular independent bookshop takes over a huge space in a Grade A-listed building designed by William Playfair – the city's architectural poster boy who also dreamt up many of the city's neoclassical highlights, including the Scottish National Gallery and Royal Scottish Academy. That gives this beautifully laid-out shop a graceful air and it's pretty much a full service affair for all your bookish needs. From bestsellers and detective fiction to history, art, cookery, crafts, gardening, graphic novels and everything in between, the ladder-bookended shelves are stacked with more novels and titles than you could enjoy in a lifetime. Look out for the author talks and events, which happen so frequently that it almost feels like an all-year-round literary festival.

2 Blenheim Place, New Town, EH7 5JH
toppingbooks.co.uk
@toppingsedin
☺

Lifestory

Even though the UK hit peak Scandi a few years ago now, our northern European neighbours still provide all sorts of inspiration for this lifestyle store which was founded long before then. The trend hunter in you will delight in hand-crafted ceramics, vases, kitchenware, jewellery, bags and wallets, and there's a department store's worth of furniture, lighting and home decor from Nordic brands – if you recognise names like Studio Arhoj, Rains, Ferm Living, HAY, Lindform and Notem, then you'll be somewhere close to Valhalla. It's not all about the northern latitudes though: local makers are also championed and there's a bean-to-barista coffee bar where you can take a break from shopping or pause before deciding what you've got room for in your suitcase or roller luggage.

53 London Street, New Town, EH3 6LX
lifestoryshop.com
@lifestoryedin

Lifestory

Valvona & Crolla

Valvona & Crolla

Who are Valvona & Crolla? For the uninitiated they're Benedetto Valvona and Alfona Crolla, two immigrant Italian merchants who set about importing salamis, cheeses and wine for the fledging Italian communities that moved to eastern Scotland in the late 1930s. Their legacy is a cave of goodies still supplied by small artisan producers from their homeland and the delicatessen is now the country's oldest – and one of its most celebrated. From humble roots, the store has become the headquarters of a mini empire – the family behind the deli now run a number of other Italian cafés and bars throughout the city – yet this original still captures the imagination best, with its diverse collection of aged Parmesans, pestos and pasta flours, honeydew honeys, truffle creams and hand-sliced prosciuttos. Besides the treasure-trove delicatessen, there's a café-restaurant, bakery and venue that's used throughout the Fringe Festival every August.

19 Elm Row, New Town, EH7 4AA
valvonacrolla.co.uk
@valvonacrolla

The Portobello Bookshop

Seaside Portobello – aka Porty, to locals – is for sunny days, but wet ones bring book lovers to this beautiful tribute to the written word in all its forms. The store was formerly a fishing tackle shop, not that you could tell nowadays, and the main space has the expansiveness of a library, with bumper floor-to-ceiling shelves, but the essence of a chatty community hub. The focal point is the cash register flanked by four Romanesque columns, then behind that are several other brightly-lit galleries for novels, coffee table books and children's stories. Author events and talks are a major lure for the community – and certainly worth checking out if you're in the neighbourhood at the right time.

46 Portobello High Street, Portobello, EH15 1DA
theportobellobookshop.com
@portybooks
☺

Bard

Scottish craft and design is having a bit of a moment, which
makes this tucked-away shop and gallery with more than
a tartan shortbread biscuit tin aesthetic to it the perfect rainy
day find. It's run by partners Hugo Macdonald and James
Stevens who love items grounded in place and their goal is to
create a sense of story in your home, be it through ornamental
bowls, vases or an antler candelabra – hence the name Bard, the
Scots' word for storyteller. The store's mission extends to what
you wear too and you can find woven merino scarves from Skye,
leather Glasgow satchels, Fair Isle lambswool pullovers and
snow beanies perfect for a wild day out in the Cairngorms.
Most of it is pricey, but all of it is sublime.

1 Customs Wharf, Leith, EH6 6AL
bard-scotland.com
@bard.scotland

Index

Managing Director • Sarah Lavelle

Commissioning Editor • Stacey Cleworth

Art Direction & Design • Emily Lapworth

Senior Designer • Katherine Keeble

Photographer • Alexander Baxter

Head of Production • Stephen Lang

Production Controller • Martina Georgieva

Artwork credit

Page 47: *Stand Cowboy Painting* by Thomas MacGregor, tdmacgregor.com

Published in 2023 by Quadrille,
an imprint of Hardie Grant Publishing

Quadrille
52–54 Southwark Street
London SE1 1UN
quadrille.com

Cataloguing in Publication Data:
a catalogue record for this book
is available from the British Library.

ISBN 9781837830688

Printed in China

MIX
Paper from
responsible sources
FSC® C020056
www.fsc.org